The Splendor of Brasstown Valley

Mountain Folks

by

Leota Hunter Hamilton

Bloomington, IN  Milton Keynes, UK

authorHOUSE™

AuthorHouse™
1663 Liberty Drive, Suite 200
Bloomington, IN 47403
www.authorhouse.com
Phone: 1-800-839-8640

AuthorHouse™ UK Ltd.
500 Avebury Boulevard
Central Milton Keynes, MK9 2BE
www.authorhouse.co.uk
Phone: 08001974150

First published by AuthorHouse 6/14/2006

ISBN: 1-4259-1935-9 (sc)

Library of Congress Control Number: 2006901600

Printed in the United States of America
Bloomington, Indiana

This book is printed on acid-free paper.

In loving memory of my beloved son,
RICKY ALAN ROGERS,
who will always be my Love, my Joy, and my inspiration.

Table of Contents

BRASSTOWN VALLEY

Deep in the heart of the Blue Ridge Mountains lies the Brasstown Valley known as the Young Harris Valley, and often referred to as the Enchanted Valley, located in Young Harris, Georgia. The valley gets its name from Brasstown Bald Mountain, highest peak in Georgia, which towers over the pristine valley like a giant encompassing it in unsurpassed beauty and tranquility. It is also the home of Brasstown Creek which roars, twists, crooks, and winds its way for many miles through some of the most scenic beauty imaginable on its way to the Hiwassee River in North Carolina.

The valley floor consists of fertile bottom land along the creek, gentle rolling hills with lush green foliage, green pastures, and small to medium sized mountains.

Brasstown Bald, and the chain of tall mountains, covered with huge hardwood trees, form a natural bowl shaped crater surrounding the unspoiled valley. Viewing the high mountains from the valley floor gives one a sense of protection from the outside world, and a deep feeling of peace, contentment, and security. No other place on earth is exactly like this valley where one can experience such an inward sense of freedom, solitude, and oneness. In the stillness one can hear the rhythms of nature in the melodies of the insects, the song of birds, the gentle rustling of the trees, and the bubbling sounds of water rushing down the streams. This enchantment is one of the reason why the valley is called the Enchanted Valley.

The valley experiences the four seasons, spring, summer, fall, and winter, with average temperatures ranging from the mid 30's to the mid 80's. Rainfall is plentiful, and it rarely snows except in the most sever winters, then maybe only once or twice, with accumulations of one to ten inches. The coldest weather occurs in the months of December, January, and February.

Springtime in the Brasstown Valley is a season of great activity. The earth begins to awaken from its winter sleep. The fragrant wild flowers nod their heads in the gently warm breezes attracting scores of honey bees and butterflies. The robins, wrens, brown thrashers, cardinals, and many other birds return with their songs of joy, and begin the work of building nests for their young. Hummingbirds dart here and there, drinking the sweet nectar of the honeysuckles, wild azaleas, and the rhododendrons.

Wild animals roam through the fields, and forest lands, in their continuous search for food, and a place to raise their offsprings. Deer are often seen eating the fresh tender grass along road sides, and in pastures. Wild turkeys, black bear, red and silver foxes, raccoons, and other animals make their home on the higher mountainsides and sometimes venture into the valley searching for food.

The valley is blessed with an abundance of food and many varieties of wild herbs. There are wild fruits such as blackberries, strawberries, dewberries, raspberries, persimmons, crab apples, plums, grapes, and many others. Much of the wild fruit is used by the Mountain Folks in making cobbler pies, puddings, jams, jellies, and juices. Most Mountain Folks live according to the law of the land, and are grateful for its bounty. The fruit is carefully gathered by hand, and care is given to the vines, plants, and trees, so that next year's harvest will be plentiful, and that there will be enough left to feed the wild animals. After the fruit is gathered, much of it is canned in fruit jars to be used later. Some of the fruit is dried in the sun and used to make delicious fruit tarts for special occasions. The rest of the fruit is usually made into jams, and jellies, using old fashion recipes that preserve the unique flavor of the wild fruit. The tradition of berry picking would not be complete without at least one of Granny's famous fruit cobblers at supper time.

The Mountain Folks' art of survival, and law of the land, has been handed down, generation after generation, since the valley was first discovered by pioneer, John Bryson, around 1835. One of their treasures, and greatest asset, is their love, and concern, for one another. If a neighbor needs help, it is provided expecting nothing in return, but also knowing the unspoken law, that the neighbor will return the help when needed, or in turn, will help someone else. The Mountain Folks are independent, grateful, and gentle people. They are friendly, wave, and speak, to everyone they meet on the roads, in the stores, and in the churches. For centuries, they have loved and cared for the land in the valley, and while they have made their living from it, they have still preserved the unspoiled scenic beauty. They always give back to the land for what they take, especially when they are in the mountains digging herbs to use in home remedies, they only take what is needed, and plant back the seed so the plants will be plentiful for next season. Home remedies, made from the herbs, have healed many common ailments, and diseases, and given much comfort to the people during their time of sickness. The Mountain Folks have a storehouse of knowledge in the use of herbs, in tonics taken at certain times of the year, to help build up the body and keep it strong and healthy. In years past, they have had to rely on herbs and home remedies, as there were very few doctors, and they were generally many miles from the valley, and their mode of transportation was usually by horseback, wagon, or carriages which could take a long time to get to the patient. In those days, most of the country doctors used herbal remedies in their practice, as herbs were more gentle to the body, and helped to keep the body strong enough to be immune from most diseases.

Wild nut trees grow abundantly in the valley and on the mountainsides. The Mountain Folks get together with their families, and neighbors, for an all day trip to the mountains to gather nuts in the fall. A picnic basket of food is carried along, with baskets and tow sacks, to hold the nuts. Wild chinquapins, and hazel nuts, are a favorite among the Folks, and many are eaten as they are picked. The wild chinkapin are dwarf chestnuts, but are much sweeter and more delicious than chestnuts, and are much smaller, and are harder to pick out of the open sharp burrs. The sharp needle-like burrs stick into fingers, and cuticles, causing them to bleed, and may be sore for days, unless a good pair of protective gloves are worn while picking out the chinquapins, and a heavy pair of leather shoes to protect tender feet from stepping on burrs.

Huge chestnut trees once grew plentifully on the mountainsides until about the 1930's, when a blight hit all the trees and killed them. Fragments of chestnuts logs, and stumps, can still be seen in the mountains where they fell, or have been cut for the lumber. The chestnut is a very hard lumber, and lasts for centuries, and the Mountain Folks lost a valuable asset when all the trees died. There are still several chestnut trees in the valley that are not native to the area which survived the blight, but the taste is not the same.

The chinkapin trees are becoming very rare due to so much land development on the mountainsides, and tops of mountains, where the developers usually cut all the trees down to provide a view for their houses.

Another favorite nut is the hazel nut, which grows on hillsides, and along stream banks. The hazel nut also has a burr, but not like the needle-like burr of the chinquapin, it is more solid surrounding the nut, and the nuts can not be successfully gathered until the burrs open in the fall. The nuts are gathered and saved for special occasions such as a great treat for Christmas, or special gatherings of the family.

Black Walnuts are the most common nut gathered by the Mountain Folks in the fall. Huge trees are scattered throughout the valley, on most family farms, and are more plentiful than chestnuts, chinquapins, and hazel nuts. When the nuts begin falling from the trees, they are picked up and stored where the squirrels can not get to them, and after a few days when the hull softens, the process of hulling the walnuts begins. A lot of hard work goes into the process of hulling walnuts as each individual nut has to have the soft hull removed by hand, and the hands turn dark brown with stain from the hulls which eventually wears off. Frequently folks are seen with brown hands at church, or shopping at the stores, and everyone knows that they have been hulling walnuts. These days a lot of the folks use rubber gloves to prevent the stained hands.

After the walnuts are hulled, they are placed in a tow sack, or baskets to dry out. After about two months the nuts are dry enough to be cracked out. Then the hard work begins. The nut shells are hard to crack, and a heavy hammer and an old fashioned flat iron placed on the lap is usually used. The nut is placed on the flat iron, with the point sticking up, and hit with a hammer, so that the nut will crack open in sections in order to pick out the large sections of walnut meat without breaking it up. If the nut is not cracked in this way, a nut pick has to be used to dig out the meat, and this results in more work, less big pieces of nuts, and takes much longer to crack out enough nuts to make a batch of chocolate fudge, or walnut

cake. There is so much work in cracking black walnuts, not to mention the mashed and cut fingers, that this day and age most people will not go through all this work, and will buy the nuts from someone else, if they can find them, and pay about $10.00 a pound for them cracked out. Black walnuts are very delicious any way they are used. A good treat is to roast them slightly, with a little butter and salt, and eat them while they are still warm. Many folks use them in walnut brittle, chocolate fudge, cookies, and cakes. A good walnut cake sells for about $20.00, or more, if you can find a charity bake sale that has one, which is very rare.

Black walnuts are a favorite among the squirrels and other small animals. The squirrels take the nuts and bury them in the ground for their winter supply of nuts, and this is how most of the trees spring up in the valley in different places.

So we can thank the squirrels for most of our native nut trees which supply us with an abundance of free wild food.

Hickory nut trees are very plentiful on the mountainsides, and in the valley, and also are a favorite nut for the squirrels, who plant most of them. Hickory nuts are sweet and delicious if you can crack out enough to get a taste. They are much harder to crack out than black walnuts, because they are much smaller. Because of this, very few folks take the time and work involved, and let the squirrels have all of them. Hickory wood is a very hard wood, and is often used in barbecue pits for the unique sweet flavor of smoked barbecue, or hickory smoked turkey. Hickory chips, and wood, was also used in smoke houses in the old days before refrigeration, to smoke the hanging sides of pork, and beef, for the winter's supply of meat. In those days all the Mountain Folks had a smoke house to preserve their meat after hog killing time.

CREASY GREENS

Creasy Greens is another free wild food that grows in the bottom lands along Brasstown creek. Creasy greens are a flat plant that grows flat on top of the ground, in old corn fields, and has shiny dark green leaves, which grows in a circle about 12 inches in diameter. The plants are ready for harvest in late winter, and early spring, and the best way to gather them is with a sharp knife blade, placed under the plant next to the ground, and cut them off. The greens have to be washed several times to removed all the grit and dirt from the bottom leaves, which grow on top of the dirt, and then are placed in a large cooking pot with a hunk of fat back, and a lot of water for pot likker, and boiled until tender. A bowl of wild creasy greens, a hunk of cornbread to soak up the pot likker, and a wild ramp, or onion, makes a unique, and delicious meal, that has graced the table of the Mountain Folks for centuries, and was probably handed down to them by the Indians, who taught them many things about wild foods, and herbs. Creasy greens have such a unique and different flavor from other greens that it can not be described, it has to be tasted to know the difference.

POKE SALET

Fried poke salet is another wild food that is enjoyed by the Mountain Folks, in the springtime. It is gathered, as soon as it starts popping up out of the earth, while the shoots are young and tender. The poke salet is washed many times, then a batter is made from flour, egg, milk, salt and pepper, then the poke salet is dipped in the thin batter, while it is fresh and green, not wilted, then placed in a skillet of hot oil, and deep fried, until golden brown. Served with leatherbritches beans, new potatoes, onions, and cornbread, and you have a meal that can not be matched anywhere. Poke is a wild herb and grows everywhere throughout the valley, in yards, gardens, fields, and along roadsides, and is free for the taking. When the plant matures, it is full of dark wine colored berries, which the birds and wild animals eat, and scatter the seed throughout the valley. Again, we can thank the birds, and wild animals, for our supply of free poke salet each year.

RAMPS

Springtime would not be complete without at least one trip to the mountains to hunt wild ramps. The wild ramp is a herb that is a member of the onion and garlic family. The Mountain Folks get together with their families, prepare a basket of lunch, and head to the cool, damp mountainsides in search of wild ramps. Wild ramps are getting hard to find, in this day and age, as so many have been gathered, and not allowed to seed out for next years crop. Some communities in North Carolina have a ramp festival each year, and many are gathered for this event, which is one of the reasons why they are so hard to find. Ramps grow in hollers, and coves, in the mountains where it is very shady and cool. Ramp hunting is a lot of fun, hard work, a lot of walking, and a great enjoyment, just to be out in the mountains in the middle of Mother Nature enjoying her bounty.

YELLOW ROOT

One warm spring morning my Dad needed some Yellow Root for one of his herbal tonics. He planned to go to Brasstown Creek in search of the wild herb, which is a shrub like plant that grows about 18 inches high, and is found in mountain areas, stream banks, and damp woods. The root of the plant is used in teas as a spring tonic, and for stomach disorders. The roots are a deep golden color.

I happen to be at the home of my parents, Melvin and Ruth Hunter, on the Swanson Farm in the valley. My dad told me that I could go with him to help dig the roots. We climbed into the old truck and headed down Brasstown Creek Road, crossed the bridge, and parked the truck to look around. Soon my Dad located a few large clumps of yellow root growing on the banks next to the creek. I was delighted at finding it so quickly, as I didn't know for sure what it looked like, when my dad pointed it out to me.

"Now we have to get permission to dig it from the land owner. You always ask permission before you dig. Most folks don't care, but its nice to ask just to be sure," my Dad told me.

We got back in the truck and turned right on a little road, and stopped at the first house on the left. Dad knocked on the door and a lady came to the door, and I was never so shocked, and surprised, as I recognized one of my good friends.

"Why, Cecile Doughty. I didn't know you and Pappy lived here."

Cecile was equally as shocked when my Daddy introduced me as his daughter.

"I've known Mr. Hunter for years, but I didn't know he even had a daughter." she told me, and then told me that my Dad and Mother used to hunt arrowheads in her fields down by Brasstown Creek. She told us that we could get all the Yellow Root we wanted, but not to dig the ferns growing on the creek banks.

I have known Cecile and Pappy Doughty for many years. We have worked on many community projects such as the Chamber of Commerce, Lions Club, Georgia Mountain Fair, and Governor Miller's Appreciation Day Dinner, held shortly after his election for Governor of Georgia. Governor Miller is also a native of Brasstown Valley, but that's another story.

Cecile and Pappy are good folks to know, and blend right in with the folks in Brasstown Valley. They are caring people, and do a lot of volunteer work in the community. Pappy is a licensed electrician, and warm air heating, and cooling contractor, dedicated to his work, and he never runs out of anything to do, and refers a lot of appliance customers to my company, Ace Services. Cecile is a dedicated volunteer worker for the Girl Scouts, and is always happy to help out in many community projects.

I would have loved to stay and talk to Cecile more, but Dad wanted to go ahead and dig the Yellow Root before it got any hotter, so we climbed back into the truck and drove to the bridge again and parked the truck. Brasstown Creek looked so cool and refreshing that I would have loved to pull off my shoes and wade in the creek. Dad started digging the first clump of Yellow Root, and as he uncovered it, I picked

it up and stuffed it in a sack. As Dad dug the roots he was busy teaching me about how to identify the herb, and many ailments that it was used for, and how to prepare the roots to make teas, and tonics. It reminded me of when I was a small child, and of all the herb medicines Dad gave us when we were ailing. We did not have money to go to a doctor for every little illness, and when we felt puny and did not have a good appetite, then Dad would make Yellow Root tea, and after a few doses of it, we had a hearty appetite, and could eat just about anything that was set before us. The tea tastes bitter, but if your stomach is nauseated, it tastes good, and clears it up right away. Some folks take it for high blood pressure, some use it as a gargle for sore throats, or sores in the mouth, cuts and bruises.

The relaxing sounds of Brasstown Creek, and Dad's soothing teaching voice, made me realize that I was having a happy and enjoyable time, and I did not want it to end, but soon Dad had enough roots and we went home. It was time to wash and dry the roots, so we found Momma's old wash tub, that I used to wash clothes in with a rub board when I was a child, before we got the first old square tub Maytag wringer washer. We put the roots in the tub, and filled it with water, and started rinsing the dirt off. After five rinses, we decided the roots were clean enough to dry. We placed the roots on a large piece of plywood in the sun to dry. After a couple of days in the hot sun, the roots were ready to be stored away. The next time I went by my parent's house, Daddy gave me a bag full of Yellow Root to take home to use, and also gave me a large dose of tea he had made in his little earthen tea pot. Herbs are better for you if the tea is cooked in a glass, or earthen, container.

Daddy has great knowledge in the use of herbs in home remedies. It was handed down to him by my grandmother, Rendie Hunter. When I was a small child, I would often go with Grandma Rendie to the woods, and mountains, to gather Boneset and Butterfly roots. My grandmother was very intelligent in mountain customs, and ways, and taught me many things about survival. She was the midwife that delivered me when I was born, and she also delivered all my little brothers. In those days women did not go to the hospital to have their babies. They could not afford the cost, even if there had been hospitals close enough to go to, and medical insurance was unheard of. So mountain women had to be tough, and skilled, in order to take care of themselves, and raise their families. They had to know how to plant crops, gardens, raise cows, hogs, chickens, ducks, sheep, goats, horses, and mules. Not only did they have to work in the fields, and garden, but also they had to do all the cooking, canning, and preserving food, make all their clothes, quilts, and necessary items, used in the home.

AUTUMN IN BRASSTOWN VALLEY

Autumn is truly the season of increase in the valley. It is a season filled with activity on the farms. The farmer's crops must be harvested at just the right time for each food crop. The corn fields, with their tall corn stalks, and plentiful ears of corn, have been drying in the warm Autumn sun, and will be ready to pick in the middle of November.

Earlier in the summer the cornfield beans, which grow up tall stalks of corn, are picked and strung, broke up into small sections, washed and packed into fruit jars, which are placed in a hot water bath canner, or a steam canner, and cooked for about 30 minutes in a steam canner, or about two hours, in a hot water bath canner. Some of the Mountain Folks are afraid to use steam canners, for fear that they will blow up, and some do. Instructions must be followed carefully in the use of steam canners, but this decreases the cooking time, and about three times as much canning can be done in a steam canner.

Many years ago, back in the 30's, 40's, and 50's, all the Mountain Folks had to can in, was the hot water bath canner. The old wood kitchen stove was fired up, and the canner placed on the hot eye, and filled with jars. Water was poured in to cover the jars, about an inch above the lids. Plenty of stove wood had to be used in the stove to keep the canner boiling for two hours. Many of the folks would put their jars in a dish pan full of water on the stove to get the jars hot enough to start boiling quicker. Heat from the wood stove in the middle of the summer's canning season could often times be unbearable, and any time saved was spent cooling off on the front or back porch with a glass of cold water, and rest for a tired body. But aching feet, and backs, are soon forgotten, as the sense of gratitude and security is felt by the "putting up" of food. It is a feeling of well being that can not be explained.

In autumn Brasstown Valley is a blaze of brilliant colors as the trees, plants and shrubs prepare to shed their leaves for winter's sleep. The scenery changes daily, and one can never see the same scene twice unless it is captured and recorded on film. It is a time when tourist visit the mountains to see the beauty, and stop to take part of Brasstown Valley's bountiful harvest home with them. They buy home canned jelly, jam, pickles, vegetables, honey, sorghum, pumpkins, apples, black walnuts, greens, collards, turnips. dried fruits, and many other foods that are available from the farmers, and roadside stands. Many hand made quilts, and other mountain crafts, are also available, and the Mountain Folks make everyone feel welcome, and are grateful for the sale of their items, as the money will be used to pay for the things they can not make or grow.

Autumn is the time that potatoes are plowed out of the ground, or dug by hand, depending on the size of the potato patch. They are then picked up by hand, and each potato is carefully examined to make sure there are not cut places on the potato that would cause it to rot after it is stored in the cellar. The Mountain Folks depend on having enough potatoes to last well into the next summer until their next potato crop comes in. By this time the potatoes that have lasted this long are sprouting, and wrinkled, and hard to peel,

but taste good just the same. Many of the farmers do not have the money to spend buying potatoes from the grocery store, and have to eat the wrinkled ones until about the middle of summer when their potato crop has grown enough for them to scratch out new potatoes, and after carefully washing all the dirt away, they are boiled in water until done. Then each potato is taken out of the boiling water, covered with butter, salted with a little salt, and lots of black pepper, placed in a bread pan or iron skillet, and browned in the oven. The new potatoes are so delicious cooked this way, that one can hardly wait until the time to scratch out new potatoes. Often new small potatoes are mixed in with the green beans and cooked. It gives the green beans an extra good taste.

Sweet potatoes, or yams, are harvested in the same way as potatoes, and stored in the root cellar, hopefully to last through the long winter. Sweet potatoes are cooked many different ways, and in the days when fireplaces had to be used for heat, and cooking, the folks would place the sweet potatoes in the warm ashes of the fireplace near the hot coals and bake them, split it down the middle with a knife, and put a slice of butter in the middle, while the potato was still hot, and this makes a good meal, or afternoon snack. Sweet potatoes can be sliced, and fried in butter, in an iron skillet, or candied, by adding a cup of sugar. Pies are often made with sweet potatoes, or better still, a good sweet potato cobbler. Also if a farmer had a good supply of sweet potatoes, some could be fed to the farm animals along with their other food.

Also, Autumn is the time to harvest the pumpkins. And back in the days before farm tractors, and trailers, came into use, the farmers would hitch up their team of mules to the wagon, and drive them through the pumpkin patch, loading the heavy pumpkins as they went. After the farmers stored all the pumpkins they needed for food to last through the winter, the rest were stored away to feed the farm animals. Cows, mules, horses, and pigs love to eat pumpkins, and this helped the farmer stretch their food supply through the long winter until the next crop was harvested. In those days not only did the farmer have to worry about having enough food to last the family throughout the winter, but he also had to worry about having enough food for the farm animals. Much hard work for the farmer went into growing enough food to feed the stock, and in turn the stock could help him by pulling the plows, pulling the wagons, providing his family with milk, butter, beef and pork, eggs and chicken, ducks, and turkey for Thanksgiving and Christmas. During hunting season the farmers would often hunt deer, rabbits, and squirrels to help with their winter's food supply. The mountain farmers in Brasstown Valley are tough, and can adept to all kinds of weather problems, and still survive off the fruit of the land. They love the land, and take good care of it as their very survival often depends on producing good crops, and keeping their land in good shape. They know from experience when to plow the land, when to plant the seeds for each crop, and when to harvest them.

OLE HOOD PLACE

I was born February 15, 1939 to my parents, Melvin and Ruth Hunter, who lived at that time with my Grandmother, Rendie Hunter. My Grandfather, William Hunter, had died in 1938, and I never knew him. It wasn't long after I was born until my parents moved to the ole' Hood Farm on Brasstown Creek. The farm was located a short distance behind the present day Blue Ridge Mountain EMC.

My first memories in life are of living in Brasstown Valley on this farm. We lived in an old "L" shaped, three room, farm house situated at the foot of a large hill. My Uncle Dwight's house is located on top of this hill, and my Grandparents, Virgil and Correan Swanson's, house and farm, was just below the top of the hill on the opposite side of the hill. Mommy, Daddy, and I walked up this hill, and down, many times when I was about two years old. My brother, Harley, was a baby at the time and had to be carried on Daddy's back, and I wished many times that I could be carried too, as my little legs would get so tired by the time I got to the top of that hill. But it was soon forgotten as we arrived at Granny's house. There were so may things to see and do and usually my cousins, Annie Mae and Harold Hunter were there to play with. This was during World War II, and Uncle Jack Swanson, my Mother's brother and Uncle Frank Hunter, my Momma's brother-in-law, had to go away and fight in the war. So Aunt Sue, Momma's sister, and the children stayed at Granny's while Uncle Frank was away. I can remember that it was troubled times for the family as Uncle Jack was reported missing in action. Granny worried so much and did not know if he was dead or alive. Soon she got a telegram telling her that he was a prisoner of war. Uncle Frank also was a prisoner of war. I, as a child, felt all this worry and anxiety, and I hoped that it would soon go away and my family would be normal again. This was around 1942 when there was a great shortage of many necessary items such as kerosene oil, gasoline, sugar, coffee, metals, and many more items needed that the Mountain Folks had to buy at the store. So many materials were needed to fight World War II, that the governments issued "ration stamp books" to each family, and only so much of the rationed supplies could be purchased at one time, and if the family ran out of "ration stamps" for certain things, then they would have to do without them. Momma still has some of her "ration stamp" books, and it has been well over 50 years since they were issued. Also, at this time, there was a great migration from the mountains to the cities. Mountain Folks, who did not have to serve in the war, were going to the cities to work in factories that had been converted to build war materials. This was a way they could serve their country, and also make a living for their families. The Mountain Folks lost a lot of their native people in this migration, as many of them never came back to Brasstown Valley. There were many family farms lying idle and growing up in trees and brush, because there was no one to farm the land.

When we lived on the ole' Hood Farm, I remember being chased by a game rooster with sharp spurs when I was about two years old. I was out playing with my little dog, in the yard, when this old rooster saw me, and started chasing me. I was so little that the rooster looked like a giant chasing me. I was scared, and ran as fast as I could screaming at the top of

my lungs for Momma and Daddy to help me. This old rooster knocked me down, pecked my arms, face, and stuck his spurs into my legs, and I was bleeding when Daddy found me and chased the rooster away. That was the last time I ever saw that old rooster, and I guess my family had him for Sunday dinner. For years after this incident I was afraid of roosters until I grew up enough to throw rocks at them if they acted like they wanted to chase me.

When I was about two years old living at the ole' Hood Farm, my Dad farmed with a yoke of oxen. I can remember riding in a sled pulled by oxen to the fields on Brasstown Creek. The oxen pulled the plows and cultivators that Daddy used to plant corn, wheat, hay, pumpkins, watermelons, and the garden. Pumpkins and watermelon rinds were fed to the oxen and cows along with hay, corn and wheat. We always had plenty of chickens, ducks, and geese which ran loose around the yard and barnyard. We had a chicken house for them to sleep in, and nests for them to lay eggs in, but many of the old hens would make their nests out in the woods and hatch out a bunch of "bitties". Baby chicks were called "bitties" in those days, and I would often find their nests and gather up the eggs. When Momma gathered the eggs she would always leave one egg in the nest, and this was called the "nest egg." The hen was supposed to be fooled by this one egg and keep on laying eggs instead of "sitting" on them. The hens would not "sit" on just one egg as they usually had at least a dozen when they started "sitting."

Momma would cook the rich duck and goose eggs for us to eat at breakfast, but most of the hen eggs were taken to the store and traded for other things we needed. We always had a good breakfast each morning with milk gravy, hot biscuits, streak-o-lean, eggs and jelly. We were a family that lived off the land, like most other families in Brasstown Valley. Daddy did not make a lot of money to buy the things we needed, so we grew most of them, or made them. But we always needed things like kerosene oil for the lamps, sugar, salt, baking soda, and shoes, which had to be bought at the store, and the eggs and chickens were traded at the store to help pay for them.

I remember one day when I was about three or four, Annie Mae and Harold, my little brother, Harley, and I were at Granny Swanson's farm playing in the barnyard. Well, one of us, I don't remember which one, had some matches in their pocket, and we started building a fire in the fireplace of our "make believe" playhouse. Our playhouse was close to the

haystacks, and we used some hay from the haystacks to make our "make believe" beds, which were too close to the fireplace. We built a tiny fire and pretended we were cooking our meals on this fire, but soon the fire caught the "make believe" beds on fire, and the next thing we knew the whole haystack was on fire. There were many haystacks stacked all around Grandpa's barn which made it more convenient to get the hay to feed the farm animals. We were plenty scared and did not know what to do, so we just started screaming, and soon Grandpa, Granny, Daddy and Momma came running from the house with water buckets. One drew water from the well at the barn, and the others ran with the water and poured it on the fire. They didn't save that haystack, but they saved the other ones and kept the fire from burning the barn down. Well, by this time, we were plenty scared. We knew we were in for it. And sure enough, Grandpa went into the house and came back with the razor strap, and gave each one of us a good licking. Not only did this hurt us, but we were hurt even worse by the stern lecture he gave us. We learned very young that matches were not to be played with, and that the razor strap could be used for other things besides sharpening the razor.

When we visited Grandpa's farm, he would often let us help do the chores. We would get to feed the chickens and also the pigs. We would shell corn, and scatter it over the barnyard for the chickens to eat. We could slop the hogs, and feed the pigs some of the pumpkins and corn. There were many pigs, all different sizes, and even some baby pigs. We did not bother them, because if anyone even came close to the baby pigs, the old sow would become angry and looked like she could tear a child to pieces. Grandpa always warned us not to get in the hog pen when the sow had babies, so we just threw their food over the fence. We always wanted to pet the tiny pigs, but we knew we had better not, as we didn't want to loose any of our fingers.

Our family went to church at Old Union Baptist Church when I was a little child. We would go every Sunday, and that is the only day that I could wear my Sunday-go-to-meeting dress. Granny Swanson made most of my clothes out of "feed sacks" and sewed them on her treadle sewing machine, because my mother has been blind for most of her life. Granny Swanson and Grandma Hunter made all the clothes my family wore except the overalls. Daddy would buy them at Mr. Hood's store, on credit, until he could make enough money to pay for them. My Daddy had a good charge account at the store, and he worked hard and always paid his debts. This is one of the valuable teachings that I learned from my parents. Always work hard, and the money that you earn, use it to pay your debts first. Then if you have any left, get what you want. This teaching has stayed with me all my life.

At that time the biggest place in Young Harris was the Young Harris College. The college was established in the valley in 1886 as a college where the poor mountain children could get a higher education without having to leave their beloved parents and the family farms where they were needed to help with the farm work. The college provided many scholarships to mountain children who could not afford to pay tuition. There was always a way for the student to work their way through school. Not only did Young Harris College provide an education for the children, but it provided employment for the parents in many families. My Great Grandmother, Millie Ann Thomas, worked at the college, and her daughter, my grandmother Correan Swanson also worked there. My mother, Ruth Swanson Hunter, was born in one of the old houses on the college campus, December 23, 1912. My Aunt Sue Hunter, and my Aunt Eldie Swanson, also worked at the college. I don't know what kind of work they did, but I imagine that it was cleaning the dorms, or working in the laundry, or dining hall. There are many folks from Brasstown

Valley still employed, today, at the College. The College is one of Brasstown Valley's greatest assets.

As poor as we were Mommy and Daddy always managed to give us children a little something extra at Christmas time. Momma would start baking cakes and cookies for our Christmas Dinner a few days before Christmas. We were always given the dough bowl to sop after each cake was mixed up and put in the oven. A few days before Christmas, we kids would go out into the woods and find the best cedar tree for our Christmas, cut it down, take it home, and we were allowed to decorate it. We strung popcorn and paper chains on the tree. We did not have regular glue to stick the chains together with, so we made a paste out of flour and water and used that to stick the chains together. We used the colored pages from the "Sears Roebuck" catalog to cut out the strips of paper for the chains. The "Sears Roebuck" catalog was very important to us. It was our "wish book" and not only OUR "wish book" but our parents also. The catalog was used to cut quilt patterns from, to make toy airplanes from, but its greatest use was in the "out house."

REVIVAL MEETING

One time when I was about four years old, Grandma and I went to a Revival Meeting, held at night, at a little church in the Friendship Community. It was a nice clear night, and I could see all the stars shinning, and hear the harmonious music of the katydids, and frogs, as we walked along. We didn't need a flashlight, because there was plenty of light from the moon to guide our way. I always went with Grandma to church, and she could find plenty of churches within walking distance for us to go to in Brasstown Valley, Friendship, and Bell Creek.

After about an hours walk, we arrived at the church. The kerosene lamps were burning brightly, and there were many of them. The windows were open to let in the fresh, cool air, and I could still hear katydids singing.

I had always been told to be good in church, to sit very still and listen to the preacher. I began to get tired from being so very still, and still the preacher preached on and on. I wanted to move, but I was afraid to. I managed to stay still a little while longer when all at once Grandma, who was holding my hand, got up off the church bench, into the aisle and started dancing around and clapping her hands, jumping up and down, and I looked around and everybody was doing it. Grandma looked so happy and so did everyone else. They were all shouting, but

I couldn't understand a word they said, they must surely be talking heaven talk, because the only word I could understand was "Hallelujah" over, and over, again. I didn't want to be left out so I started jumping up and down, and clapping my hands and repeating "Hallelujah". I decided right then that this was the church to come to. Everybody could be happy at this church and didn't have to sit so still. The shouting and excitement went on for a few minutes more, when all at once someone jumped on my bare feet, and I let out a shriek which no one heard, and began crawling through legs, and found the nearest bench I could climb up on. I held my aching toes and made a decision right then, that the next time I went to Church, I was going to wear my shoes.

WASH DAY

Back in the early 40"s before the days of electricity and indoor plumbing, washing clothes was a major task. Water was drawn out of the well and poured into the cast iron wash pot. A fire was built around the wash pot to heat the water. Several large wash tubs were required. Two for rinsing the soap out of the clothes after they were washed, and two for the actual washing. Two rub boards, and two bars of homemade soap, or Octagon soap if a family could afford to buy it, were required for the two "washing tubs". Hot water from the wash pot was carried and poured into the two "washing tubs" and tempered with cold water until hands could survive the hot water without being burned. Then the wash pot was again filled with cold water to heat.

Usually the white clothes were washed first. The "washing tubs" were filled with several towels and linens to soak. Each piece of clothing in the tub had to be washed one at the time. Each piece of clothing was pulled up onto the rub board, soap rubbed over it, and then the rubbing began. Up and down, many times, the piece of clothing was rubbed on the wash board and dowsed in the water of the tub, and after inspecting the piece of clothing to make sure it was clean, it was then wrung out by hand and put into the rinse water tub. After rinsing through two tubs of water, the clothing was then ready to put into the wash pot to boil. The boiling killed germs and helped to bleach the white clothes, and linens, to a sparkling white. After the white clothes were lifted from the wash pot with a clean stick and put into a tub of cold water, the water was wrung out of each piece by hand. Next the dresser scarfs, pillow cases, white shirts, blouses, table clothes, and any other decorative household item was starched by each separate piece dowsed in the tub of starch water and wrung out. The clothes were then ready to hang on the clothes line. Each piece of clothing was fastened to the clothes line with clothes pins, and left to dry in the fresh air and sunshine.

The homemade starch was made before the washing began, as most people could not afford to buy "store bought" starch. They made it themselves by using a portion of flour, depending on how stiff they wanted their clothes, and adding water, probably a couple of quarts, and then boiling it on the wood cook stove until it thickened. It was then thinned with water before use.

After all the white clothes were washed, it was time to wash the colored clothes. The shirts, dresses, blouses were washed the same way as the white clothes. Next came the heavy overalls with all the brass buttons and metal fasteners on the shoulder straps. When these were wet they were very heavy and awkward. After they were rubbed a few times on the rub board, and soap applied, they were taken to the "battling block" and hit over and over again with the "battling stick" to loosen the dirt and help clean them. A "battling block" is made from a tree trunk sawed to a length of about 30 inches and stood up lengthwise. The "battle stick" is made from a piece of lumber and formed into a paddle. In using the "battling block" on overalls, one had to be careful not to hit the metal buckles and buttons with the "battling stick" or they would be bent out of shape and would not fasten when the overalls were put on to wear.

Also, the "battling stick" could serve two purposes at the same time. If one was angry and upset about something, they could take out the frustration on the "battling block". it might not be too good for the overalls, but certainly made one feel better about having to work so hard trying to keep someone's clothes clean, and having skinned, raw knuckles from the rub board, and wrinkled hands to go along with it.

After the clean clothes hung on the line all day in the fresh mountain air and sunshine, they were taken into the house and the clothing that did not require ironing was neatly folded and put away. Sometimes a sprig of scented lavender was folded into the bed sheets and towels to make them smell even better.

The starched clothing that was worn as well as the household decorative items had to be ironed. Some of the starched items had so much starch, and were so stiff, they could stand up alone. Before the starched items could be ironed smooth, without wrinkles, they had to be dampened by slinging a few drops of water on each piece, then rolling it into a tight ball so the water would dampen the clothes evenly, until they could be ironed. While the clothes were being dampened, the flat irons were set on the wood cook stove to heat. The iron was tested to see if it was hot enough by wetting a finger, and quickly sticking the finger to the hot surface of the iron, and if it made a hissing sound, then the iron was hot enough to begin ironing. The Mountain Folks always had more than one iron, because when the iron cooled down on the dampened starched clothing, it had to be reheated on the stove. Sometimes before a garment could be completely ironed, two or three heated irons had to be used.

Usually the Mountain Folks would pick one day a week for washing clothes, and the next day was set aside for ironing. If it rained on wash day, then the washing was put off until a clear day so the clothes could dry on the clothes line. If an afternoon thunder shower happened on wash day, or it looked like it was going to rain, the clothes were quickly taken off the line and rushed into the house before they got wet. If there were enough members of the family where one could iron while the others washed, the slight damp clothes were removed from the line and ironed immediately. The clothes ironed much smoother, and this saved all the work of dampening the clothes and waiting until the next day to iron. The Mountain Women were very particular about their laundry. Each item had to be "spic and span" clean, starched and ironed, especially their Sunday-go-to-meeting clothes and their children's school clothes. No child was allowed to go to school with dirty clothes. Every day when the children came home from school, they had to change into their "everyday" clothes to do their chores, or to play, because very little money was available to buy school clothes, or cloth to make clothes. There were many "feed sack" dresses, shirts and blouses made in those days, because the Mountain Folks ripped open the beautiful print cloth sacks that chicken fee, or cow feed came in, and made clothing for their families, curtains for their home, or pieced quilts for their beds.

STRAWTICKS AND FEATHERBEDS

Many decades ago, in Brasstown Valley, many folks used strawticks filled with clean fresh straw as a mattress for their beds. They used heavy canvass to make their strawticks, and sewed them by hand, or by a treadle sewing machine, if they happened to have one. The cloth was cut the size of their bed, sewn around the four sides, and a split was made in the middle of the strawtick for the purpose of stuffing the straw into the tick.

Every day when the bed was made, the straw in the tick had to be fluffed up by hand through the slit in the middle so that the person sleeping in the bed would be more comfortable, and the bed would be smoother. Often, as the straw packed down and became lumpy, the straw had to be replaced with fresh straw. Usually to make the bed more comfortable, and warm, a featherbed was used on top of the strawtick.

In those days all the fine soft plumage of geese, ducks, turkeys, and chickens were plucked and saved for featherbeds and pillows. These small feathers were called "down". These feathers were usually plucked in the hot summer time, and it was not unusual to see many geese, and ducks, running around the barnyard with naked breast and rear ends.

In those days each time a chicken, or barnyard fowl, was butchered for special occasions, the folks plucked the "down"

and saved it. Usually they built a fire under the wash pot, and filled it with water, and after the water was boiling, they took the chicken and dowsed it many times in the boiling water. This killed the germs on the chicken, and cleaned the feathers, and made it much easier to pluck the feathers. After all the feathers were removed, then the chicken had to be "singed" over an open flame to remove the tiny hair like feathers before the chicken could be washed again and cooked.

It was an old custom to have a chicken dinner on Sunday if one had invited the preacher and his family to dinner. Sunday dinners were always good, and special, and the whole family was usually present to enjoy them. The Mountain families always had close, loving relationships with their families and their friends. They taught their children to love one another, to love their neighbors and friends, to respect their elders, and to get a good education. They were taught to help out in any situation without expecting anything in return. And many times they have heard from their parents, " If you can't say anything good about somebody, then just don't say anything." When this good advice was followed, a child seldom ever got into trouble at home, or at school. And if a child did get into trouble at school, and got a spanking, then he could expect another spanking when he got home. Mountain children were taught discipline, and how to discipline themselves so as to know what to do in any given situation. They were not taught " What is always good for the goose is good for the gander." This kind of thinking could get them into deep trouble in many situations. They were taught the Golden Rule, "Do unto others as you would have them do unto you", and when this rule was followed their lives were harmonious, loving, kind and innocent.

MUSKRAT HIDES

Among the many small animals that lived on the banks of Brasstown Creek were the Muskrats. A muskrat is a large, essentially aquatic, fur bearing, North American rodent with a long, scaly, sparsely-haired tail, partially webbed hind feet, and a musky odor, and also the Muskrat is covered in beautiful brown fur.

The fertile bottom lands along Brasstown Creek were planted with corn, soybeans, wheat, rye, pumpkins, watermelons, sorghum cane and many other food crops. The Muskrats could do a lot of damage to the farmer's crops by digging up the fresh planted seeds and eating them, and when the corn crops matured, and had dried ears of corn on them, the Muskrats would tear down the stalks of corn, take the ear of corn and feed it to their young.

The Muskrats, in large numbers, could virtually wipe out a corn crop if the farmers did not fight back with their own unique ways of controlling the Muskrats. One of the ways was to set steel traps, and trap them in fall and winter when they could not find a lot of food to live on. The traps were set along the creek banks close to their den. The Muskrats made their dens by swimming just under the water's edge and burrowing up into the creek bank just above the flowing water,

and raised their young in these tunnels where other predators and animals could not get to their young.

The farmers would wrap up in warm clothing each morning and "run the trap lines." If the farmer was lucky, and there were a lot of Muskrats, the farmer could catch as many as a half a dozen, or more, each time he "ran the trap lines". The Muskrats were killed with a rock, or large stick, while they were still in the trap. Then the farmers would take the Muskrats home, skin them, and stretch the skin-with the skin outside-on a large wide board to dry.

When the farmer had a sufficient number of hides, and these included fox hides, coon hides, and if he was very lucky, sometimes mink hides, the hides were then taken to Jake Plott in Blairsville, Georgia to be sold. Jake Plott owned a large hotel on the square in Blairsville, and he was also a dealer of animal hides, and Ginseng herbs. The Ginseng herbs were exported to China where they were used in medicinal teas. The hides were sold to other dealers, and used to make fur coats.

Money was so scarce in those days that many families depended on the money from the sale of Muskrat hides, and the hides of other small animals, to buy their winter shoes. In those days a pair of shoes had to last the children through the cold winter until it was warm enough for them to go bare footed, and they often had to be bare footed until November, or until the family could get together enough money to buy their shoes. After the shoes were worn through mud, snow and ice, the soles began to come loose from the shoe, and it wasn't unusual to see a child with a can rubber over his shoe to hold the sole to keep it from flapping when he walked. A child was taught to take very good care of their boots, and shoes, as well as their overalls, and dresses. They kept their boots greased with axle grease, or meat skins, so the leather would not become hard and crack. A lot of water, rain, and snow could seep through those cracks and cause the foot to become very cold, and no one wanted frost bitten feet from walking in the snow.

The hides from Muskrats, Mink and Foxes were a blessing to many families as it enabled them to provide needed things for their families that they could not afford, otherwise. Also the trapping helped to control the pests to keep them from eating up the farmer's crops.

RABBIT BOXES

Hunting rabbits for food was a way to help stretch the winter's food supply. Fried rabbit makes a delicious meal when served with soup beans, baked potatoes, and cornbread. Many families depended on rabbits, squirrels, and deer for their fresh meat in the cold winter time.

One way the Mountain Folks had to hunt rabbits was to make rabbit boxes out of small pieces of old lumber. They were easy to make and a child could make them. After the child finished with the rabbit box, they carried the boxes and set them in rabbit trails. Rabbit trails could be found in old fields, that had not been used during the year, and allowed to grow up in weeds and grass, and they could also be found in cow pastures, or in the woods. After a good rabbit trail was found, the rabbit box was then baited with bits of apple peelings, carrots, or cabbage, and left for the rabbits to find. Every day the child checked his rabbit boxes, and bragged to his friend and family about how many rabbits he had caught. This made the child feel real grown up by being able to help out with the family food supply. Throughout the winter, many rabbits were caught this way, and became food for the family dinner table.

Some families raised rabbits in cages and sold them on the market for food. Feeding the rabbits and taking care of

them often became a chore for the children.. Most often the children did not want to give up the rabbits when it came time to sell them, because they had become pets, and they each had individual names. But the children knew their families had to make a living the best way they could, and the rabbits had to go. If a family killed a child's pet rabbit for food, then they could depend on the child not eating any rabbit for dinner, and being sad for days at the loss of their rabbit.

Making a living in Brasstown Valley in the 30's, 40's and 50's was very hard. It was a time when there were very few cars, and trucks, and most families walked to town, and church, or rode in wagons, carts, sleds, and buggies driven with mules, horses, and sometimes even oxen. If a family had a nice buggy to ride in, they were considered to be rich. At this time there was one store in the valley owned and operated by M.C. Hood located in the Jacksonville Community. Mr. Hood, a very good and generous person, was loved by the folks in Brasstown Valley. His store provided many things the Folks needed such as salt, sugar, nails, hardware items, bolts of cloth, leather goods, shoes, flour, sacks of feed in beautiful print colors, rice, barrels of pickles, hoop cheese, needles, thread, plows, seeds, and even candy and chewing gum. It was a child's delight to be able to visit Mr. Hood's store with their families, because Mr. Hood always gave the child a stick of peppermint to suck on, and it was always sucked on to make it last as long as possible. Later on, there was E.L. Brown's General Merchandise store which is still in business today, and Cable's store which stayed in business as long as Mr. Cable was alive. In those days most children believed a person owning a store was very rich, indeed. But what the children did not know was that most of their families had a charge account at these stores, and were allowed to charge for their supplies, and things, until their crops came in. The store owner often received their pay in eggs, chickens, livestock, fresh vegetables, and many other things that the families could exchange for the things they needed to raise their families.

CORN SHUCKING

Many years ago, in Brasstown Valley, many families would have "corn shucking" after their corn had been harvested in late November. All their neighbors, and friends, would pitch in and help shuck the corn to feed the livestock. All the corn was shucked, and shelled, by hand and it would take a long time to shuck and shell a crib full of corn. There were sometimes as many as 15 to 20 corn shuckers working per day and all these workers had to be fed. Many of the wives of the corn shuckers would help to cook dinner for the corn shuckers and then wash up the dishes by hand after the meal. In those days water had to be heated on the wood stove and poured into two dish pans, one for the washing and one for the rinsing, then all the dishes had to be dried with a drying towel and put away until the next meal.

After each ear of corn was shucked, it was put into a bin for the shellers to shell. After the corn was shelled, it was put into tow sacks, and made ready for Townsend Mill to grind into meal. All the farmers in the valley used Townsend Mill to grind their meal, as it was conveniently located in the middle of the valley. A dam was built in Brasstown Creek, and a big water wheel was used to turn the big mill rocks that ground the meal. Cornmeal, and buckwheat flour, was ground at the mill. The farmers used mules and wagons to take their grain

to the mill, and some even carried a sack full and walked to the mill. This was heavy and hard work in those days, but if a farmer didn't yet own a horse, mule or oxen, then he carried the bag of grain on his shoulder to the mill. And if the farmer did not have a horse, mule or oxen, the farmer often had to swap out work with his neighbors in order to get his fields plowed for the Spring planting. Most of the time it did not take long for a farmer to get livestock to help with the farming.

Before the cornmeal could be made into cornbread, it had to be sifted to remove all the outside husks. the bran was then tossed into the hog slop to feed the hogs. When folks made cornbread, they used a greased iron skillet to cook it, and put it in the oven of the wood cook stove. In less than 30 minutes, the bread was brown and ready to eat. Many suppers meals consisted of cornbread and milk, and many families were grateful to have this.

After the corn shucking was over for the family, then the family was expected to help shuck their neighbors in exchange for their work. There was never any money charged for this service as it was always returned when anyone needed it. In those days money was scarce, and almost impossible to earn as everyone lived off the family farm, and grew all their food, made their own clothes, furniture and other things they needed. The families may not have had a lot of money, but they were rich just the same. They had love for one another. They had compassion for their neighbors, and friends. If any neighbor needed food, herbs for sickness, clothing, wood for their fireplace, or their fields plowed or cleared, the mountain folks shared what they could without compensation. They knew in their time of need, the favor would always be returned many times. The Mountain Folks felt responsibility and love for their neighbors and friends, and had to depend on them for many things. They were far richer in having these things than just having money, because in those days there were not many things in Brasstown Valley to buy.

LEATHERBRITCHES

Leatherbritches are dried green beans. Many of the Mountain Folks of today still make leather britches beans. Green beans that are not fully matured make the best leather britches. Usually a fully matured green bean hull will burst open and loose the bean while it is in the drying stage. Its better to use the green beans when the bean is about half mature.

To make leatherbritches beans, the fresh beans are picked, and strung, and left whole. After they are carefully washed, the whole green beans are strung on a long string, usually with a needle and thread, and hung in the house, or on the porch, until the hulls and beans are completely dried, at which time they are ready for use. Some folks put them in a clean cloth sack and place in their freezer. They will keep for years in the freezer, and bugs will not get in them if they are later taken out of the freezer and stored somewhere else.

Some folks break their beans, dry them in the sun, and then put them in the freezer until use. Either way, leather britches are very delicious when cooked.

To cook leather britches, take as many beans as you need for a meal, put them in a pot, and put about three inches of water over them, add salt to taste, and season with a ham hock. Boil the beans until hulls and beans are tender, adding water each time they boil down, for about two to three hours. Makes a delicious meal served with cornbread and other vegetables.

SAUERKRAUT

Every summer in Brasstown Valley during canning season the Mountain Folks would make their Sauerkraut. Sauerkraut is made from cabbage from the vegetable garden.

The task of making Sauerkraut usually began early in the morning, and it was usually a job done by the women. Several large heads of cabbage were brought to the kitchen, and the outside leaves were taken off, and the cabbage carefully washed. The cabbages were chopped by hand in a wooden bowl with a double edged cabbage chopper. This was a task that could take several hours depending on how many cabbages were used. After each cabbage was chopped very fine, the bowl was emptied into a large dish pan and left until all the cabbages were finely chopped.

The next step was to wash a large clay butter churn, or wooden barrel, to store the Sauerkraut in while it was making. After this, a layer of cabbage was placed in the bottom about an inch thick, and salt to taste was added. This process was repeated until the churn or barrel became full, or until all the cabbage was used. Then a saucer was placed on top of the cabbage, with a clean large stone on top of the saucer, to hold down the cabbage while it was making, then a clean, white cloth was tied over the top of the churn, or barrel to keep the Sauerkraut clean. Usually after about three or four days, the Sauerkraut was made and it ready to can.

JELLY MAKIN'

Among the Mountain Folks, in Brasstown Valley, are many jelly makers. Some still use old fashioned recipes which have been handed down from generation to generation, but these recipes require more cooking time for jelly to set, depending upon what kind of fruit juice is used. If the juice and sugar are not cooked the right amount of time, or to the right consistency, the jelly will not set, and will become syrup which is alright if you like syrup. After the jelly is poured into jars, cooled and still has not set, it can be recooked by adding a cup of water or juice and a cup of sugar. Boil until the juice dropping from a spoon starts to thicken on the last drop, if it does not drop off the spoon you can assume that the jelly is ready to pour into the jars. A further test is to pour a teaspoon of the boiling jelly onto a cold plate, and after a minute if you tip the plate and the jelly is thick enough not to run off the plate, it is ready. Set the jelly off the heat for a couple of minutes, take a big steel spoon and skim off the foam, before pouring jelly into jars. A good way to prevent having so much foam to dip off is to add one teaspoon of margarine to the jelly before it starts boiling.

OLD FASHIONED
BLACKBERRY JELLY

To make Wild Blackberry Jelly, first you have to find a patch of Wild Blackberries. They grow in all sorts of places, on the edge of yards, on banks of roadside, in old fields, in the woods, on banks of Brasstown Creek, and other streams, or in cow pastures. One needs to dress in a long sleeve shirt, a pair of thick trousers, knee boots and a straw hat. As it is usually very hot when blackberries get ripe, it is best to pick them early in the morning, or late in the evening. Blackberry briars grow very thick, and the thorns can be very painful when they stick into hands, scratch and cut exposed hands and face. And it is best to use a little insect repellent to keep the "chiggers" away, and be sure to watch out for snakes which may be hidden in the berry patch.

When you start picking the berries choose only the large, ripe and plump berries that have turned black. When you have your bucket full, take home and wash them through at least two waters while carefully looking at each berry to make sure no leaves or bugs are on them. Then put them in a boiler, cover with water just above the berries, and allow to cook until berries are soft, then after they cool a bit, strain berries through cheese cloth, and wring out all the juice into another container. Now you are ready to make jelly:

Four cups of juice
Four cups of sugar
One teaspoon of margarine

Place juice, sugar and margarine in a boiler, and boil until the right consistency, when the last drop remains on the spoon when testing it, it gets thick when a teaspoon full is dropped into a cold plate and does not run off the plate when tipped. Set boiling jelly off heat and allow about two minutes before skimming the small amount of foam from the jelly. Pour into jars and seal immediately, then turn the jar up side down for five minutes, then turn right side up. Check the next day to see if jelly is set, and make sure each jar is sealed.

Long ago when Mountain Folks made jelly, they sometimes used paraffin wax to seal their jelly. The wax would be melted and poured onto the top of the jelly which made a tight seal against the glass jar. Then it was ready to store in a cool, dark place, such as a root cellar until the family was ready to eat it. Most of the time the jelly would be used up in a matter of a few months.

Back in Great Grandmother's day, after the jelly was poured into jars, it was sealed simply by placing a clean piece of paper on top of the jar and tying a string around it. After the jelly had been stored in the root cellar for a few months, it would begin to mold on top, but the Mountain Folks still used it anyway. They just dipped deep into the jelly jar, removed all the mold, and the rest of the jelly was still good.

In more recent times jelly is usually made using fruit pectin and following the directions and recipes that are inside the box which tells how much sugar, fruit juice, etc. and how long to cook it. Less cooking time is required, and if directions are followed correctly, the jelly will set well after it has been poured into jars and allowed to cool, if it doesn't set, it can also be reprocessed.

CHERRY JAM

One day toward the end of May 1993, a good friend, Ruth Carlisle, and I decided we wanted some cherries. Ruth wanted to make cherry pies, and I wanted to make some cherry jam. So we went to an old orchard which had a few cherry trees with cherries on them. We picked all that we could reach standing on the ground, but it was not enough to do what we wanted, so Ruth climbed up the tree and picked the ones that we could not reach from the ground. It was a sight to see her in the top of that cherry tree, and I hoped that she would not fall out and break a leg, or get hurt. Ruth is the wife of A.J. Carlisle, whom I met in the Towns County Lions Club. We all do volunteer work at the Georgia Mountain Fair on the many Lions Club projects each year.

After we finished picking all the cherries we could get, Ruth went home to make her pies, and I went home to make jam. First I washed the cherries through two waters, then I took out all the pits. Next I put the cherries in a blender and chopped them. Then I was ready to make the jam:

    4 cups chopped cherries
    4-3/4cups sugar
    1 pack Sure-Jell
    1 teaspoon margarine

I took the sterilized jars from the dishwasher, and placed the can lids in boiling water so they would be hot when time to put them on the jars. I measured the chopped cherries, 1 teaspoon margarine, and poured them into a boiler. Next I measured the sugar, saving 1/2cup to mix with Sure-Jell. After I had mixed 1/2sugar cup with Sure-Jell I poured the chopped cherries and Sure-Jell into a boiler, and brought to a full rolling boil which could not be stirred down, then I added the remaining sugar and brought to a full rolling boil, and cooked for 2 minutes. I removed the boiler from the heat and allowed it to cool for about 2 minutes, then I skimmed the small amount of foam from the top and the jam was ready to pour in the jars and seal. I had enough cherries to make two recipes of jam which totaled 18 half pints. The Cherry Jam was so delicious and such a pretty red color that I planned to make more next year. Jam makes nice gifts for friends.

During the summer another good friend of mine, Sandy Bell, and I decided to make some jelly to sell. Sandy had never made jelly before and thought it would be lots of fun. It was fun working together, but Sandy did not know how much hard work goes into jelly making. The hardest part is getting the fruit, especially if you use wild fruit. We wanted wild blackberries so we picked all that we could find, and blackberries were hard to find this year because of the three month drought in May, June and July 1993. With berries that we picked, and 5 half gallons of juice I had stored in my freezer, we made over 100 jars of Wild Blackberry Jelly. We also made blueberry jelly, and gooseberry.

My parents, Melvin and Ruth Swanson Hunter, have several bushes of pink gooseberries that grow in their yard. They gave them to me and I picked two gallons of gooseberries. I used one gallon to make jelly and stored the other gallon in the freezer to use later. After Sandy and I prepared the fruit and took out the juice, we had about 30 jars of delicious jelly to sell. Sandy also picked two gallons of blueberries from a farm near Blairsville and put them in her freezer to use later for jelly. When we made our blueberry jelly, we used the Sure-Jell Light recipe where more juice and less sugar is used. This recipe brings out the real blueberry flavor.

We sold a lot of our jelly at the Georgia Mountain Fair's Country Store this year. The fair was held in August and again in October. We did not sell as much in October, but this is the first year for the October Fair and not as many people knew about it. Some of the flavors of jelly we have are: Wild Blackberry, Blueberry, Gooseberry, Gooseberry Butter, Red Currant, Black Plum, Red Plum, Peach Jam and Cherry Jam.

"TIGER"

One by one they fall, gently and delicately, to the ground. Each is a beautiful picture of life, individually patterned and shaped, falling by the millions, yet no two are formed alike. Each flake in itself is a world of its own, here to stay only a moment, in its white splendorous glory. Each is surely a magical gift from the heavens forming a new world of white glorious silence.

The flakes cling to the branches of every tree turning them into a beautiful world of their own. Each tree delighting in their new appearance knowing that never again will they experience the same flake as their laden branches bear and knowing that each flake adds a beautiful scene to be experienced only for short time.

Nowhere in this beautiful silent world is there to be seen an animal, bird or insect. Only the trees, shrubs and the snowflakes.

The valleys and mountains are like waves and ripples in an ocean of white floating in their silent world, as flakes by the millions invade their privacy with a glorious splendor, as if by magic, they create a whole new world.

The birds and wild animals are hidden in their nests and shelters, patiently waiting for the flakes to stop falling. They sense that it would be useless to try to find food in this blizzard.

As soon as the snow stops falling they will be everywhere looking for bits of food to carry them through the storm.

The date is February 18, 1979. I am thinking of all the baby quails that scratch and eat the seeds and insects in my yard. I stand looking through my window and watch them as they are busy moving from one place to another in my yard looking for food. I crumble up bread crumbs and food scraps and wade into the snow which covers 8 inches of my boots as I take the food to the same place in my yard and scatter it out for the wild animals and birds. I look in the snow and see tracks of something at this site. I believe these tracks belong to a large bird as they appear in the snow and lead only a short ways and then disappear completely. At one end of the tracks it looks like wing prints in the snow as if the bird tried to balance itself in the deep snow.

I make a daily habit of feeding the wild animals the food scraps which are left from our meals. Many animals enjoy these scraps. I know because I put them in the same spot each time. I have seen tracks from rabbits, foxes, ground hogs, possum, squirrels, deer, and bears. There is a huge old owl which resides in a tree close to the feeding spot. I hear him at night as he sings to the dark world. I have often seen him perched on the tree limb above the feeding site. Once I saw him eating the food through my window. I don't see the animals very often, but I know they are not very far away. I know they miss me when I am away from home, as they come to eat and there is no food for them. I see their tracks where they have been there.

About a year ago a huge wild cat would come and eat the scraps. I noticed that the cat would come everyday looking for food. I started putting out saucers of milk for him, which he truly loved. He was a beautiful cat with long back legs and jumped like a rabbit when he ran. His fur was a brown and yellow stripe. I thought he was a bob cat, but yet he did not have a tail, only a little fluff like a rabbit. I looked in World Book Encyclopedia and saw a picture that looked like him with a description "a very rare cat from Ireland, a Manx. Only a few have been brought to America.

Each day I would move the cat's cup of milk a little closer to the house. I would watch him through the window as he drank the milk. One day I waited quietly on the porch while he drank his milk. I talked to him softly and told him not to be afraid, I meant him no harm. He would look up at me and meow. I named him "Tiger" because the stripes reminded me of a tiger.

I kept feeding the cat and talking to him softly each day. I would try to feed him at the same time each day and saying "Tiger, come get your food." Soon I would hear him answer from the woods with great "meows", and could hear him running through the dead leaves in his haste to get his milk. He could run faster than any cat I have ever seen run.

I worked with this cat until he finally came close enough for me to reach out and stroke him while he drank his milk. By this time he was large and very fat. He would wind himself around my legs, around and around, purring ever so contentedly, while he made the circles around my legs, rubbing his great body against my legs, as though he was thanking me for the food. He was still wild and afraid of everyone else. I was the only one who could pet him. He seemed to know that I meant him no harm. When I wanted to see him, the only thing I had to do was call "Tiger, where are you?" Where ever he was, if he heard me, he would always answer me and quick as a flash he would be there.

My cat had several narrow escapes from hunters with guns who thought he was a Bob Cat. A lot of people knew that I was working with this cat and left him alone. I tried to tell everyone I saw about the cat and not to shoot him, that the cat was not a Bob Cat.

One weekend about 9 months after I had been working with the cat, I came home from Atlanta and immediately started calling him. This time he did not answer or come when I called. I had a sinking feeling in the pit of my stomach that I would never see the cat again.

By this time I had grown to love this cat very much. I looked forward to seeing him and talking to him. He would look at me with his huge blue eyes and seem to understand every word I told him. He would let no other person come near him as he was still quite wild. My husband, Lee, was afraid of him and the cat sensed this. The cat would arch his back "blow" at him if he even came near him.

One day we left the back door open and I placed his milk in the kitchen and called him. He came into the house, very much afraid. After I continued talking to him, he calmed down and drank his milk. Lee said something to me at this time and frightened the cat and he ran into my bedroom and went under the bed. He lay on the soft carpet and refused to come out when I called him. I didn't know how I was going to get him out of the house. He was a very dangerous cat if you caged him in a tight spot. His claws were very long and he had very strong teeth.

Before I started trying to tame the cat, Lee and Charlie, had built a trap out of chicken wire and caught him in the trap. He was so wild and frightened that he bit through the chicken wire trying to get out. I felt sorry for the cat and made them turn him loose. I think this is the reason the cat did not like Lee and Charlie.

Going back to the time the cat was in the bedroom, Lee decided that he would get the broom and try to scare him out from under the bed. Lee was down on his knees looking under the bed and moving the broom under it trying to get him to move. The cat disappeared and when I looked up the cat was on the bed, arched and "blowing" and ready to jump on Lee's back. I told Lee not to move, and I gently talked to Tiger and finally coaxed him out the back door. This was the last time I invited the cat into the house.

I found out two weeks later after I called him and he did not come that he had been shot by my neighbor, whom I had forgotten to tell about my cat. My neighbor thought he was a Bob Cat and said he was fooling around his chicken house. I knew that the cat was after rats around the chicken house.

I thought my heart would burst when I first heard the news that "Tiger" was dead. I felt so guilty for taming him and knew when I was not home he would try to find food wherever he could. He was an excellent hunter and kept all the rats and pests out of my garden and yard. We had lots of rats around the shop and "Tiger" frequently visited the shop, and I have seen him many times in my garden with rats in his mouth.

I know that the wild animals must get very hungry in a snow storm such as this, but I have learned a lesson from this experience-don't try to tame or feed wild animals. I still keep my bird feeder full of seed especially in snow storms such as this one when the birds can't find food because of deep snow.

GREAT BLIZZARD OF 1993

Crooked Creek Community is located in the north west corner of Brasstown Valley and is accessed by Crooked Creek Connector off U.S. Highway 76 East, and by Crooked Creed Road off Highway 17 and 69. This part of the valley has natural rolling hills, lush green pastures with livestock, two fruit orchards, small streams, and a chicken farm. Birds and wildlife are abundant in this small valley as well as wild flowers and many varieties of wild herbs, blackberries, walnuts, persimmons, hickory nuts, blueberries and some wild strawberries. The mountainsides and valley contain hardwood trees of every variety, and pine trees.

This small valley is home to several residents; the Hamiltons, the Heusels, the Chastains, Don Kimsey, and a few other kind neighbors. The valley is quiet and peaceful with very little activity other than the occasional noise of the chickens, bellowing of the cows at feeding time, or the shrill cry of the Red Tail Hawks which have their nesting grounds on the hill above the Hamiltons. Many small wild animals roam through the Hamilton's yard in their search for food. The squirrels frequently rob the two bird feeders and scatter the seen on the ground which the birds eat in company with the squirrels. The birds don't seem to be afraid of the squirrels, but if the neighbor's cat comes along, if frightens them and they all fly into the trees.

Friday, March 12, 1993, dawned the same as most other days. The clouds were low and puffy, and the temperature averaged about 40 degrees. About 1:00 pm on my way back to work from lunchtime, I noticed a misty white cloud hovering around Brasstown Bald. I looked at the mountains on the opposite side of the valley and saw the same misty white clouds hanging over the tops of the mountains, I knew it was snowing. I had heard the report on TV that a snow storm was coming our way, and it was expected to snow about 6 inches.

The evening wore on and down in the valley where I was working it was misting rain. I could see Brasstown Bald through my window, and the white clouds had thinned out a little. After 5:00 pm I went to my mother and dad's home and cooked supper. My parents, Melvin and Ruth, Lee and I ate supper, cleaned up the kitchen, then Lee and I went home. I was watching the 6:00 news program which showed a News Crew up on Brasstown Bald who were showing the snow coming down. They expected 24 inches, and said they would be spending the night there.

I went to bed about 9:00 as I was tired from the days work preparing income taxes. I looked out the window and saw that the yard was getting white and snow was coming down in small flakes. I went to sleep and awoke some time in the night, I didn't know what time it was, and I noticed that I was very cold. I noticed that the night light was not on. I flipped the switch, there was no electricity. I looked out the window and could see about 6 inches of snow on the roof of our garage, and large flakes were continuing to fall. A strange feeling of anxiety swept through my body, I thought, we've had it now. I hope we don't freeze to death. Our house is total electric with no back up heating system. I was cold so I went back to bed and back to sleep.

The next morning when I awoke the house was very cold and the first thing I wanted was a hot cup of coffee. I looked out the window and saw at least 12 inches of snow on the roof of the garage. The scene was very beautiful with snow sticking to every tree limb and shrub, it looked like a frozen winter wonderland.

I still wanted a hot cup of coffee and Lee ran some water out of the hot water faucet which was still fairly warm and poured it over coffee grounds, but it was a poor substitute for perked coffee and tasted awful.

This day was Saturday, March 13, and it felt like a day to stay in bed as it was very cold in the house. Soon the wind began blowing with gusts up to 60 and 70 miles per hour. This made the temperature even colder, and I knew it was useless to even think about trying to walk out to a neighbor's house who had heat, so we stayed in bed almost all day. We had canned tuna fish and crackers for lunch. For supper we had peanut butter and jelly crackers with milk.

It was so cold in the house that we were wearing two pairs of pants, two sweaters, two pairs of socks, and gloves which we also wore to bed. The wind was blowing so hard that I just knew that any moment a tree would come crashing into the house or garage. I heard a loud noise upon the roof and heard something fall, and I was afraid to look. When I did look I could not see anything and began to think what could that be. I thought of the TV antenna. I immediately went to look and saw the TV antenna lying up against the house with a couple of wires still holding it in place.

We had a small battery radio and listened to a radio station out of Murphy, North Carolina until about 8:00 am when they lost their electricity. The only other station we could get was in Chattanooga, and they were in the same situation as we were; no electricity and it was still snowing. We tried to call our local Blue Ridge Mountain EMC throughout the day, but the lines were always busy. We were later to learn that electricity was out in all 5 counties.

We put four heavy quilts and two blankets on our bed. We went to bed and stayed warm with body heat. My nose kept getting so cold that I put my head under the covers and made a tent so I could breathe. Every once in a while I had to have fresh air so I uncovered my face for a bit, then my nose would get cold, my throat hurt breathing the cold air, so I went back under the covers. I slept restless that night, waking up every two or three hours. I was so tired of staying in bed that my body ached all over.

When daylight came on Sunday morning I was up. I grabbed two blankets and headed for the living room couch. Looking out the window I could not believe what I was seeing. On top of the little round picnic table on the back deck was a little over 30 inches of snow. I looked for the wooden half barrels that hold the flowers in summer and they had completely disappeared. I have a little antique wood stove in the yard that I use as a planter for flowers, the snow was up to the top rim around the top of the stove and only the stove pipe was visible. I felt really frightened. I finally was able to reach the EMC about 8:00 am and reported that we had no electricity, that our house was total electric, and we had no heat. The lady sympathized with me and said to use supplies sparingly. She could not tell us when the electricity would be back on as so many trees were down on the power lines. They were literally having to cut their way into places and use bull dozers to pull their trucks into some of the places especially on the mountain sides and tall hillsides.

The wind had died down by Sunday morning and it had quit snowing. I wanted some hot coffee, and Lee tried to rig up something to make it with. He found a wire rack, and used our candle in a jar, and a small stainless steel pan to hold the coffee. He ran the water over the coffee grounds, poured it into the stainless steel container, and set the container on the wire rack which had the candle in a jar under it. After a while the coffee was hot and he poured it into a cup that was so cold that it cooled the coffee down until it was only luke worm. That was the worst coffee I know I have ever tasted in my life, but at least he tried, and I appreciated it very much.

The storm had completely caught us off guard and we were not prepared. I began thinking about the propane gas grill that used to sit on our back deck, which had been taken to the garage and stored; because last summer we had planned to build an extra room where our deck is located. I also knew that the propane tank had been carried down to Ace, our family business in Jacksonville community to be used to check out used gas ranges for sale to the public. Also, I thought of the gasoline welder with a generator on it which was at our ornamental iron shop down the steep hill from our house which was at least 1000 feet from us. I also knew that there was no way of getting it to our house, that it was too heavy to manually carry in the snow which was about 30 inches deep, and knew also that we had no vehicle that could possibly travel in this deep snow.

To get rid of the fear thoughts I was having I began to count my blessings for the things that we had. Our home which provided a good shelter for us and it was well insulated. We had several hand made quilts that Granny had pieced before her death in 1989 at the age of 94. Through all that was happening we still had telephone service and could call our loved ones and neighbors to find out how they were surviving. We still had water because in years past we had hooked up to the Towns County Water supply and disconnected our well which had an electric water pump. We were grateful for the water even though the pressure was low and hoped that it would stay on and not freeze as the temperature outside was 4 degrees. Inside the house it felt like it was in the single digits. I began thinking about the EMC linemen who were working out in the most severe weather conditions anyone ever remembered, and I knew that they were working around the clock to restore electricity to everyone. I mentally praised them and hoped that they would take precautions against frostbite and my heart went out to them for having to work in such conditions. In my heart I mentally knew that our local Blue Ridge Mountain EMC is one of the most valuable assets that we have in the Brasstown Valley, and I knew that I would never take this valuable service for granted again.

I kept wondering what the situation was like outside our little valley, as we had no local communications except our telephone. I knew it had to be bad from talking to friends and relatives. In all the calls we made and all that came into us, no one had electricity, and none of the roads, except US Highway 76 had been plowed. The only vehicles that were able to travel had to have chains, or they were four wheel drive vehicles. Our neighbor, Don Kimsey, called to check on us. He was in the same situation as we were with no heat. He had a four wheel drive pickup in his carport but his house is located down hill from our road and he had not tried to get the truck up the steep driveway. He felt it would be impossible at that time to move the truck.

It was still early Sunday morning and very beautiful outside. The sky was clear and it had quit snowing and the sun was shining brightly. We opened the kitchen door and where the sun was shining through the glass storm door it was warmer than it was in the house. So we left the door open. I was so cold that two toes on my left foot were numb. I couldn't feel anything in them. I decided immediately that I would try to walk down the hill to my sister-in-law's mobile home, about 900 feet away from our house. She had called us the day before and told us that she had propane heat and a propane cook stove and wanted us to come to her house so we could get warm and have some hot food. I knew that walking in the deep snow that I would need some support of some kind. I remembered Papa's walking cane which was in my library in the basement of the house. I made my way down the spiral steps into the dark basement, felt my way to the corner, found the cane and went back to the kitchen. I felt like some hot soup would make me feel better and help me to thaw out, especially my numb toes. I went through the cabinets gathering up some cans of vegetables, tomatoes, cut green beans, green peas, some celery, onions, bell pepper and put them all in a plastic grocery bag. I grabbed the bag, the walking cane, and started out into the snow. Lee was in front of me and told me to walk in his tracks, making it easier to walk. I tried to do this but soon found out that his legs must be a lot longer than mine or he was in a bigger hurry than I was. With my heavy leather knee high boots I could hardly lift my legs high enough in the snow to stay in his tracks. The snow came above my knees and I was loaded down with my shoulder bag, into which I had put some of my favorite books, the other hand was loaded down with the bag of food and the free hand held the walking cane for which I was very thankful for as it kept me from sliding and falling down in the snow. We had made our way down our asphalt driveway and were even with her mobile home when proceeding across I suddenly fell into the ditch of snow waist high. I did not think about the ditch being there as the snow was so level. I soon found that I could not step this high and I could only push the snow with my legs as I held the cane. I was thankful that the steps were only a few feet away. I was completely exhausted and out of breath. As I climbed the two short steps into the mobile home everything started to turn green, my head was swimming and I could not see. I spotted a chair close by and fell into it, put my head down between my legs until my ears stopped ringing and my eyes cleared up. By this time Darlene had put a hot cup of coffee into my cold hands and I drank it gratefully and asked for more. After I had drunk three cups of coffee I began to thaw out and Darlene placed a dish of blueberry cobbler in my hand. It was very good being the first hot food that I had eaten since Friday.

I gave Darlene the bag of food that I had brought and realized I had forgotten the most important ingredient, the ground beef. It was still in my refrigerator at home, but she had some in her refrigerator and made a big pot of hot vegetable soup which was very satisfying and nourishing. It felt so good to finally be warm again with a full stomach. As the evening wore on there were helicopters touring the area. D. J., Darlene's grandson, decided to write "help" in the snow, but the helicopters did not come back in our direction again. Tommy, my nephew, was beginning to worry about how much propane gas that was left in the tank. He sent D.J. to look and he came back and told us there was 15%, so we knew there would be enough to last through the night and hopefully tomorrow. Darlene asked us to spend the night and made up a twin bed for us in an unheated bedroom, they only heat the living and kitchen area. We sat around and talked for awhile by candle light and soon everyone went to bed. A little later I heard the helicopter flying over us and our little valley. It flew to the top of Swanson Mountain where there is a subdivision with probably 35 homes. I guessed that it must be the National Guard lifting in supplies to someone who was in serious need. It hovered over the mountain top shining its lights for what must have been at least 5 minutes, then it left. We had heard earlier that night on the Murphy radio station that our own Governor Zell Miller, a native of Young Harris, had toured the area in a helicopter to assess the damages. He had called the National Guard, Red Cross, and others to help us in the disastrous emergency situation we were in, and for this we were very thankful.

I finally went to sleep and awoke early the next morning and my whole right side felt frozen where I had to lay against the mobile home wall in order for Lee and I to fit in the small twin bed, but we made it. I got up before anyone else and made my way in the dark to the living room-kitchen area and made myself a cup of hot coffee with the flash light. I sat in the dark until daylight when everyone else got up and had their coffee.

They day started out with a clear sky and sunshine. Darlene made some hot pancakes and bacon for breakfast which we heartily ate. We heated water on the gas stove and washed up the dishes. I went to the window and looked out at the herd of cattle in the pasture below us and knew that they must be very hungry as Mr. Shook had not been able to get his vehicle in through the deep snow to feed them.

I looked at the Heusel's chicken houses and the roofs were still in place, but I knew that the chickens had not had water or food since midnight Friday night when the electricity had gone off. The feeder troughs were run by electricity and the water came from a well with a pump run by electricity. I hoped that the chickens would not bunch up and suffocate.

We had kept in touch with Don, our neighbor, and told him where we were and asked him to pick us up if he managed to get his four wheel drive truck out of his steep driveway up onto the road. By this time the snow had melted a little next to the ground and he managed to get his truck near the top of the driveway and skidded off into his yard. He had called someone to come and pull him out, and he wanted Lee to help him cut some pine trees which had fallen over the road between us and his place. Lee and D. J. walked over the hill to Don's and all of them together cut up and removed four or five trees from across the road. By this time the other vehicle had arrived to pull Don's truck onto the road. He went out to check on his Father in Bell Creek Community and promised to come back and get us.

In the meantime D. J. had checked the gage on the propane tank and it was down to 10%. Tommy started to worrying about it running out and that they would be left without heat or a way to cook. We told them they could ride out with us when Don came back in.

One of Darlene's daughters who lived in Young Harris was very worried about us and had contacted the local fire department. They sent a Lady Fire Fighter in a light four wheel drive jeep to pick up Darlene, Tommy and D. J. The jeep made it fine until it reached the small hill in a curve right next to our shop on Crooked Creek Connector where it slid into a ditch and was stuck. Darlene, Tommy and D. J. walked to the jeep where it was stuck, took shovels and dug it out. They had to back the jeep about a quarter of a mile up a hill until they could find a place to turn it around.

By this time Don managed to get around the stalled jeep and pick us up. We followed the jeep out the road to Crooked Creek Road where the jeep went in the direction of Warne Highway and we went in the opposite direction toward Highway 69. There was one lane on Crooked Creek Road which had been plowed, and we managed to travel it without any trouble.

On the way I could not believe my eyes at the sight of pine trees down across the road which had been cut away so that traffic could get through. There was one mobile home with a tree across the end of it, there were pine trees still caught in the electrical wires, and a little further out the road we could see the EMC Linemen working in a pasture below the road and their truck was stuck in the snow. They had worked on the end of Crooked Creek Road all day trying to restore power. I understood then why everyone was without power.

We made it to Young Harris and I got off the truck at Swanson Road, climbed the four foot snow bank left by the plows and walked past my Mother's house on out to Uncle Dwight's house where my parents were staying. I was relieved to find out my parents, Uncle Dwight and Aunt Eldie were surviving the situation, and were actually better off than I had been. They had no electricity, but had a wood heater and a wood cook stove. They were without water as they have a well with a pump, but they melted snow on the heater to wash dishes and flush the toilet. One of the neighbors brought in their drinking water.

Lee had asked Don to take him on to our business, Ace Services, in the Jacksonville Community to check and see if everything was alright. When he walked from Highway 76 to Uncle Dwight's house, he told me that the electricity was on at the office, that the office was warm and that everything was alright.

We decided to spend the night at Mother's house as there was not enough room at Uncle Dwight's house, so we walked back to Mother', and were, once again, in a cold house. We decided to walk down to Gibson's Restaurant and eat supper before it got dark. We had a good meal and were walking back when one of our friends, Harold Copeland, riding by on a four-wheeler cycle stopped and asked us if he could give us a lift. He could ride one at a time on the back of his cycle, but when I looked at it I decided it wasn't that far to walk. He then told us about the death of one of our neighbors and dear friend who had died from running a gasoline generator in the basement of his home on Bailey Road. I was really shocked and hurt by this news and wondered why he did not think of carbon monoxide poisoning from gasoline fumes in the house.

That night I talked to my son, Ricky, and he told me that he had gotten his truck out and wanted to come and get us so we could stay in his warm house as he had a kerosene heater and electricity. We decided to stay at Mother's and told him we might call him in the morning to pick us up.

It was cold in Mother's house and getting dark by this time so we lite the kerosene lamps and found Dad's flashlight in case we had to get up during the night. The bed was warm with several quilts also made by Granny. I slept good and sound that night when my feet finally got warm.

We awoke the next morning and Lee called Ricky who met us at the end of Swanson Road and took us to his house for breakfast and a good hot shower. I had stuffed a change of clothes into a plastic bag and carried them with me all this time hoping to find someone who had electricity and a hot shower. I can't remember ever having a hot shower that felt so good. It was wonderful to be clean again and shed the two pairs of pants, socks, and sweaters that I had worn since Friday. After that Ricky took us to work. When trying to climb the four foot snow bank my feet went all the way to the bottom of the snow bank and I was once again frozen and dirty and finally managed to get to the front door and inside where it was warm and cozy.

The day was Tuesday, March 16th. Business was slow that day, and I finished up the long tax return that I had been working on the week before the snow. A customer called and wanted us to fix an electric dryer, and we told him that we were without transportation and he agreed to bring the dryer to us as he had a four-wheel drive vehicle.

By this time it was lunchtime and Lee decided to walk up to Big D's next door which was about a block from us. He brought back a couple of sandwiches, soft drinks and candy bars which were very delicious. About this time the customer with the electric dryer on his truck backed through the high snow bank and the customer and Lee took the dryer off the truck to repair it. Just then Lee remembered that his hand tools were in his truck at home, so the customer was willing to take him home to get them. They went up our steep driveway and made some good tracks in the snow and we knew that we would be able to get our vehicle to work the next day.

While Lee was getting his tools, he checked the house and found that the electricity was back on and it was warm in the house.

As the afternoon wore on about 3:00 Don picked us up to take us home and Lee told him that a snow plow had plowed Crooked Creek Connector and that we might be able to drive in from the Highway 76 side as we normally do. On this trip I noticed about a dozen pine trees that had fallen across the toad and had been cut out of the way. We made it fine until we got to the hill just before Don's house and had to stop. There were still two trees across the road which were tangled up in the electrical wires which no one dared to touch. We had to turn around and go back out to take the back road, Crooked Creek Road, into our home.

Don's four-wheel drive truck traveled up our steep driveway without trouble. We were finally home in a warm house, cooked a good hot supper, and slept in our own bed once again. I think that was the best night's sleep I'd had in weeks.

We drove our vehicles to work the next morning without any problems, up and over the tall snow bank which was melting. Business was still slow that day as many people were still without electricity. We heard on the radio that the EMC hoped to have everyone's electricity back on by Friday. By Saturday there were still people without electricity. The EMC removed the trees from the wires on Crooked Creek Connector and we were once again able to travel it. By Sunday, March 21st there were still patches of snow in our yard and on the mountain tops.

Throughout this blizzard people were lovingly helping one another without expecting anything in exchange, and often not knowing the person's name. It filled my heart with joy to see this and to know that whatever kind of emergency that may happen, that the Mountain people will be there with love in their hearts reaching out to help in any way. This will keep us all together, and we will be able to meet and solve any situation that happens.

COMMUNITY HERO
CENTENNIAL OLYMPIC
TORCHBEARER

This historic time in my life all began the first week of December, 1995. I had baked four walnut cakes and took them to the Towns County Chamber of Commerce for the bake sale they were having at Brasstown Valley Resort during the Mountain Country Christmas. I delivered the cakes and Kay Raymond, Executive Director for the Chamber handed me an application "In search of America's Community Heroes to carry the 1996 Olympic Flame" and told me to sign it and attach the article that Joan Crothers, Towns Sentinel, had written about me in November, 1995 to the back of it and mail it because this was the last day to mail it.

The following article was attached to the back of the application:

"COMMUNITY PERSON"
by Joan Crothers, Towns Sentinel Editor.

"Leota Hamilton is one person who, when she sees a need, does something about it. There was a need for a Chamber of Commerce in Towns County so she helped organize that, became a charter member and stayed in

the position of Secretary-Treasurer for five years. The Leota Hamilton Award for Extraordinary Service was created in her honor.

When Zell Miller was elected governor, many people in this area said, "I'd sure like to see THAT inauguration!", never dreaming that they could. Leota worked on that committee, calling and arranging and coming up with three tour buses full of proud area residents who were able to go to the inauguration, the Governor's Mansion for dinner, and the music show afterwards at the Civic Center. She was also there helping with the organization of the group from Towns County who went to the Zell Miller Parkway Dedication, a bus to his second inauguration and the Miller Christmas Celebrations at Young Harris Elementary School in 1990 and 1994.

Because her mother and aunts suffer from Macular Degeneration, a disease that causes blindness, she joined the Towns County Lions Club in 1988. She was only the second woman to join and is the first to be on the board.

In addition to the Chamber and Lions Club, Leota is a member of the Top of Georgia Toastmasters Club, the Towns/Union Homebuilders Association and the Mountain Computer User Group.

Last year when the TV relay station on Bell Mountain went out, Leota helped organize a group of concerned citizens who raised enough money to get something more permanent for this important facility.

Leota has been married to Lee Hamilton for 36 years, helps him with his Ace Services at their home on Crooked Creek Connector, and also has her own office doing tax returns in the little community of Jacksonville. This is a business she's been doing since '67.

On a personal note, Leota has been an intern mentor with the Prosperos School of Thought for the past seventeen years. It is an accredited, educational correspondence school that "teaches you how to think". She credits the school's basic teachings in helping her cope with life and especially her very busy life."

On February 2, 1996, I was very busy on my computer doing tax returns for my many clients when the UPS driver rushed in my office with an overnight package. He said, Hurry up and open this. I think you are an Olympic Torchbearer, and I want to know. I have delivered three of these packages this morning." I opened the package and the following letter was in the package:

"Dear Leota:

Congratulations! You have been selected as a Community Hero Torchbearer for the 1996 Olympic Torch Relay. In honor of the outstanding contributions you have made to others in your community, I would like to personally invite you to carry the Olympic Flame, the most sacred symbol of the Olympic Movement.

For 84 days, beginning April 27, the 1996 Olympic Torch Relay will bring the Olympic Flame to thousands of communities across America. You have been selected by a panel of community leaders from your region as one of 5500 individuals who will represent the best of their community by carrying the Olympic Flame.

Please read the enclosed information carefully. It briefly explains the 1996 Olympic Torch Relay and the important role you will play as a Torchbearer. The final page is a Confirmation of Participation that must be completed and returned no later than February 5. Once you have confirmed your participation in the Torch Relay, we will forward more detailed information regarding the Torch Relay in general, and the specifics regarding your Torchbearer segment.

On February 15th. communities across the country will announce the names of their Torchbearers. You will be contacted by a member of the Torch Relay Task Force in your area about an announcement ceremony to be held in or near your residence. After we receive your Confirmation of Participation, we will send you a special Atlanta 1996 Olympic Games T-shirt for you to wear to this event and during subsequent media activity.

I hope you will accept this prestigious honor to participate in the Olympic Movement and carry the Olympic Flame. I look forward to your response and your involvement in the 1996 Olympic Torch Relay.

With best regards, I am

 Sincerely,
 William Porter Payne,
 President and CEO
 The Atlanta Committee for the Olympic Games"

In all my life I don't think that I have ever been more surprised at receiving such good news. I was shocked as I had completely forgotten about sending in the application. But such an honor to be chosen as one of the Community Heros across the nation to carry the Olympic Flame in my own community was almost more than I could even dream about at this time.

On February 9, 1996 I received a memo from Debbie L. Davis, Regional Judging Panel Coordinator inviting me to come to the Georgia Mountain Center in Gainesville, Ga. on February 15, 1996 for the public announcement and media session. I immediately called Joan Crothers and invited her to go with me. She drove her car and took me to the center for this important day which also happened to be my birthday. What better birthday gift could a person have than this?

After a nice drive we arrived at the Mountain Center at 10:30 am and I registered and Debbie Davis said to me, "I know who you are from your picture in the essay article Joan wrote."

All the North Georgia Torchbearers were invited to this event, and each one was called up on the stage individually while Debbie read each essay and how each one qualified as a Torchbearer. There were many news media with cameras with flash bulbs popping everywhere during this time. We were given an official Olympic T-shirt to wear and individual pictures were made of each of us, and we were later sent one of these pictures as a gift and an opportunity to purchase more of them to give to our friends and for publicity purposes.

From Towns County there were six Community Heros chosen: Stan Raymond, Rick Martin, and Stephen Smith from Hiawassee, and from Young Harris, were Dr. Thomas Yow, Kirk Vardeman, and Leota Hamilton. One of the Torchbearers, Rick Martin, dropped out due to circumstances beyond his control.

On March 27, 1996, I received the following letter from Secretary of State, Lewis A. Massey:

> *"Dear Leota:*
>
> *Congratulations on being named an Official Olympic Torchbearer for the 1996 Centennial Olympic Games! Georgia is beaming with pride and enthusiasm as the host of the Games, and we are delighted to have you participate in what will be the most memorable Olympics in the history of the Games.*
>
> *As a Torchbearer, you represent the finest in business and civic communities throughout the state. Your leadership and dedication are to be commended, and I know you will represent Georgia with honor.*
>
> *Best Wishes for a successful 1996. The spotlight will be on Georgia, and I am glad that you will play a key role in our hospitality to the world.*
>
> *Sincerely,*
>
> *Lewis A. Massey*

It was a great honor to receive this letter and it encouraged me to practice even harder. I wanted my body to be ready for this great event and I went to the Georgia Mountain Fair parking lot each day for a fast paced walk around and around the parking lot for at least an hour carrying an iron pipe that weighed four pounds. My body began to slim down, my legs and arms began to be much stronger and the exercise made my body feel much better and I began to experience more energy.

On June 17, 1996 I received an invitation from the Coca Cola Company to visit the Coca Cola Olympic City for a special event for Torchbearers. I received two tickets and invited Joan Crothers and she drove her car to this very special event. Coca Cola had closed the park to the public for this special event. Torchbearer, Stan Raymond, and his wife, Kay Raymond, also attended this event. There was a special ceremony in which Governor Zell Miller welcomed all Georgia Torchbearers to this event, and presented a proclamation to Doug Ivester, President and CEO of the Coca Cola Company, proclaiming June 25th as Official Torchbearer Day in Georgia. Mayor Bill Campbell was presented with an official Olympic Torch, and several city council members were recognized who have worked very hard for the Olympic Games. Also, recognized was Coretta Scott King.

After the ceremonies we were free to tour the Coca Cola Olympic City and there were so many things to see such as games, baseball, track & field, gymnastics, mountain biking, paralympic wheelchair sprint, a Ronald McDonald Play Area, 100 years of Olympic history, and World record theater and in-park entertainment. The Coca Cola dancers really put on a good show and the Olympic Spirit was felt throughout the theater. One of the Coca Cola employees handed me a Coca Cola pin, a collectors item, and I purchased more Torchbearers pins while I was there. One of the great things about this event was that all the food, drinks and entertainment was free to the Torchbearers who also received an official Torchbearer Relay Team T-shirt. I had my picture taken with Doug Ivester and he let me hold the official proclamation. I also had my picture made with Mayor Bill Campbell, and Alvin Dollar, City Council member, and even had a picture made with the famous Ronald McDonald. This was such a happy and memorable event that I will always remember this day.

On July 16, 1996, just after midnight the Olympic Torch Relay Team arrived in Hiawassee, Ga. I wanted to attend, but I knew I must rest before I had to carry the torch at 5:07 am that morning in Young Harris, Georgia, my home town.

I was so excited and did not sleep well and was awake every hour until 3:00 am when I had to get up. I set the automatic coffee maker for 3:00 am and hurriedly dressed. I had one cup of coffee before I had to be at the Goolsby Center at the Young Harris College at 4:30 am. I arrived and all the rest of the Community Heros were there as well as escort runners and Share the Spirit runners. We boarded the bus and received instructions, signed releases, and received our Torches which had our running number on the end of them. We were given our running numbers to stick on our official Torch Relay uniforms furnished us by the Coca Cola Company.

It was quite dark outside and also very foggy, but it was amazing at the people who were there to cheer us on during our run.

Dr. Thomas Yow, President of the Young Harris College was runner No. 1, who started his run at the Goolsby Center on Hwy 76 and ran to just past the Blue Ridge Mountain EMC. Dr. Kirk Vardeman, our local veterinary at the Hiawassee Animal Hospital received the flame and ran to just past the entrance to Old Union Baptist Church, where I received the flame and was "keeper of the Sacred Flame" on the path down the hill along side my family's farm. This was an excellent choice for me and meant so much to me to be able to carry this flame by the family property. The family farm was originally the farm of pioneer John Bryson and Jane Bryson. John and Jane Bryson were my great-great-great grandparents who cleared the land, built a log cabin and made their home on this historic hillside in Brasstown Valley around the year of 1832. Legend handed down through the generations of my family was that John Bryson traded a rifle for the farm, and a pony to the Cherokee Indians. The first log cabin with lean-to built around it was converted to a barn and is still standing. The second log cabin that my mother, Ruth, grew up in was a one room log cabin which over the years other rooms have been added to it, and mother's brother, Uncle Dwight, lives in it today. John Bryson in his will left the farm to his daughter, Martha Melvina Bryson Swanson, and her husband, Issac Swanson, who were my great-great grandparents. Issac Swanson left the farm to his son, Jewell Oliver Swanson and his wife, Easter Canzada Keener Swanson, who were my great grandparents. Jewell Swanson left the farm to my grandparents, Virgil and Correan Swanson. The largest part of the farm and buildings is now owned by Uncle Dwight Swanson. My mother owns the part of the farm that is next to Highway 76.

I still do not know how the Coca Cola Company, who sponsored the Torchbearers Relay Team, knew where to select my Torchbearer route, but they could not have picked a better place that has so much meaning for me to run. I wondered if it was Governor Zell Miller who told them. He is a native of Brasstown Valley and knows my life history and the history of my family. He has worked closely with Coca Cola Company and the Torch Relay Team and was there to welcome the flame in Los Angeles. Governor Miller is a good friend and supporter and has encouraged me to keep writing, and he once told me that he had never seen the type of leadership provided in Towns County as the community leadership that I have been providing for the last 15 years. I have never received any pay for my community work as far as dollars and cents are concerned. But the blessings and spiritual rewards that I have received from doing this work in my community can never be bought with dollars and cents. The love, trust, and support of my community are treasures to me and could not be purchased with any amount of money.

I know who the great volunteer workers are in Towns County and have enjoyed working with them to accomplish many good things for our community that our tax dollars did not have to pay for.

When the Coca Cola Company sent me the Torchbearer flag, they said to find someone who is very important to you to wave the flag so the Torch Relay Team bus would know where to let the Torchbearer off the bus to begin their run. I chose my daddy, Melvin Hunter, who was age 91 to play this important role for me. Dad and Mother proudly waved the Torchbearer flag for me to begin my run.

When I got off the Relay Team bus, there was a large crowd of people and supporters to welcome me. It was dark and the Relay Team was so fast that I hardly got to recognize them all. But some of them were: Joan Crothers, Towns Sentinel Newspaper; Johnnie Foster, her sister Nancy and her husband whom I grew up with; Anita Dolan; my parents; my husband, Lee Hamilton, my cousin, Candace Beck who took some fabulous pictures; my friend Dominick and his lovely wife, Alicia, who also took good pictures; my sister-in-law, Kathy Hunter, and many, many more.

At last the great historical moment of my Torch run began. I was so excited and beaming from ear to ear on the half-mile, 7 minute fast walk down the hill to pass the sacred flame to runner No. 4. My escort runner walked on the right side of me and the motorcycle on the left. I have never walked so fast in my life, and was thankful for all those practice days at the level six parking lot at the Georgia Mountain Fair, and thankful that I had been carrying the heavy iron pipe on my practice walks. The three and one-half pound Torch was beginning to get very heavy before I finished the Torch run. At the end of the Torch run there was a crowd of people congratulating me, and I was handed an arm full of red roses by Jeffrey Beck, my cousin. Some of those who were at the end of the Torch run were: my Aunt Mildred Dyer; her grandson, Jeffery and her granddaughters, Hollie and Brittany; her daughter, Candace; some of the others were Susie Kimsey and her sister; Margaret Dendy; Mazy; Dominick, his wife Alicia; Dorothy Puett; and many, many others. The Relay Team bus was there to pick me back up and I wasn't able to recognize everyone. I really do appreciate them for being there so early in the morning which was a little after 5:00 am.

This was a great day in the history of my life, one that I will never forget. A day that I was able to be a part of the Atlanta Centennial Olympic Games as one of the 5500 Community Heros, selected by United Way to carry the sacred Olympic Torch right in my own community that I love so much.

At about 9:00 am on this day, my daughter-in-law, Jo Anne Hamilton, who works for Federal Reserve Bank in Five Points in Atlanta called me and told me that the bank wanted a picture of me holding the lighted flame to put in their monthly magazine and they were holding up the magazine until they could get the picture. I immediately unloaded the film from my camera which Candace Beck had used to take the pictures with and took them to the one hour film service, all the while praying that there was a good picture of me with the lighted flame. When I picked up the pictures, I was astounded at how good they were, and there was one very good one with the lighted flame. I immediately called Jo Anne at the bank and told her I would bring her the pictures. She had given the bank an interview about me a few days before and they also wanted a picture of the two of us.

I arrived in Conyers, Ga. about 5:00 pm at Jo Anne's home. She immediately started trying to locate someone with a polaroid camera to take a picture of us with the Torch. She finally found someone about 9:00 in her neighborhood and we got the picture.

When I arrived at Ricky Hamilton's, my step-son's home, he told me that we are really going to celebrate tonight with a steak supper and chocolate cake. It was really delicious and after supper we enjoyed their hot tub which I really needed for my sore legs which really got cramps in them before the night was over.

This story of my Torchbearer history was written for my scrapbook which was made and presented to me by my granddaughter, Kellie. I will treasure it forever.

www.ingramcontent.com/pod-product-compliance
Lightning Source LLC
Chambersburg PA
CBHW031259280526
45784CB00004B/1919